HOME-COOKED MEALS

Favourite Asian Dishes and More

Allan Albert Teoh

The publisher wishes to thank C S Tay Foods Pte Ltd for their support.

Editor: Lo Yi Min
Designer: Bernard Go
Photographer: Ng Chai Soong

© 2019 Marshall Cavendish International (Asia) Private Limited

Published by Marshall Cavendish Cuisine
An imprint of Marshall Cavendish International

All rights reserved

No part of this publication may be reproduced, stored in a retrieval system or transmitted, in any form or by any means, electronic, mechanical, photocopying, recording or otherwise, without the prior permission of the copyright owner. Requests for permission should be addressed to the Publisher, Marshall Cavendish International (Asia) Private Limited, 1 New Industrial Road, Singapore 536196. Tel: (65) 6213 9300 E-mail: genref@sg.marshallcavendish.com Website: www.marshallcavendish.com/genref

Limits of Liability/Disclaimer of Warranty: The Author and Publisher of this book have used their best efforts in preparing this book. The Publisher makes no representation or warranties with respect to the contents of this book and is not responsible for the outcome of any recipe in this book. While the Publisher has reviewed each recipe carefully, the reader may not always achieve the results desired due to variations in ingredients, cooking temperatures and individual cooking abilities. The Publisher shall in no event be liable for any loss of profit or any other commercial damage, including but not limited to special, incidental, consequential, or other damages.

Other Marshall Cavendish Offices:
Marshall Cavendish Corporation. 99 White Plains Road, Tarrytown NY 10591-9001, USA • Marshall Cavendish International (Thailand) Co Ltd. 253 Asoke, 12th Floor, Sukhumvit 21 Road, Klongtoey Nua, Wattana, Bangkok 10110, Thailand • Marshall Cavendish (Malaysia) Sdn Bhd, Times Subang, Lot 46, Subang Hi-Tech Industrial Park, Batu Tiga, 40000 Shah Alam, Selangor Darul Ehsan, Malaysia.

Marshall Cavendish is a registered trademark of Times Publishing Limited

National Library Board, Singapore Cataloguing-in-Publication Data

Name(s): Teoh, Allan Albert. | Ng, Chai Soong, photographer.
Title: Home-cooked meals : favourite Asian dishes and more / Allan Albert Teoh ; photographer, Ng Chai Soong.
Other title(s): Favourite Asian dishes and more.
Description: Singapore : Marshall Cavendish Cuisine, 2019. |
Identifier(s): OCN 1083049546 | 978-981-48-4129-0 (paperback)
Subject(s): LCSH: Cooking, Asian. | LCGFT: Cookbooks.
Classification: DDC 641.595--dc23

Printed in Malaysia

In loving memory of my late parents, especially my mum, Madam Ong Su Wha, who shared her recipes with me, taught me how to cook and showed me the importance of family and love.

Contents

Foreword 6
Acknowledgements 8
Introduction 10

12 SOUPS

Lotus Root Soup with Pork Ribs 14
Chicken Soup with Burdock Root and Mushrooms 16
Soto Ayam 18
Rasam 20
Sup Kambing 22

24 VEGETABLES

Acar 26
Cucumber Raita 28
Chap Chye 30
Stir-fried Ladies' Fingers 32
Spinach Curry 34
Sayur Lodeh 36
Crispy Vegetarian Yam Ring 38

42 POULTRY & MEAT

Chicken Curry 44
Chicken and Chinese Mushroom Stew 46
Port Wine Chicken 48
Rosemary and Thyme Roast Chicken 50
Ayam Masak Merah 52
Pork Belly Slices 54
Braised Pork and Yam Slices 56
Fried Bakwan 58
Rendang Daging 60
Roasted Orange Lamb Chops 62
Mutton Keema 64
Satay Goreng Kambing 66

68 SEAFOOD

Sweet and Sour Prawns 70
Gulai Kunyit Udang 72
Prawn Fritters 74
Asam Fish 76
Fish Head Curry 78
Baked Salmon with Herbs and Honey Butter 80
Steamed Flower Crabs in Bean Paste 82
Stir-fried Squid with Chinese Chives 84
Sotong Masak Hitam 86

88 RICE & NOODLES

Nasi Ulam 90
Baked Rice with Prawns 92
Luncheon Meat Fried Rice 94
Abalone Porridge 96
White Bee Hoon 98
Kampong Fried Noodles 100

102 DESSERTS

Green Bean Soup with Sago, Sweet Potato and Coconut Milk 104
Glutinous Rice Balls in Osmanthus Ginger Syrup 106
White Chocolate Blueberry Tart 108
Pulut Tai Tai 110
Rose Coconut Ladu 112
Gendang Kasturi 114

Glossary 116
Weights and Measures 120

Foreword

We first met Allan over 20 years ago when he came on board to coach at Sam Leong@Forest Cooking School. As we watched him conduct a class for the first time, it became clear to us that he had a deep passion for cooking and baking. He taught with confidence and brought new dimensions to every dish. During his time at our culinary school, Allan spoke from experience and was generous in giving students his insights and tips.

Today, Allan's generosity and love for cooking continue to reach many through his books. After writing several baking cookbooks, Allan has finally written a cookbook that features savoury dishes, and we couldn't be more excited. While Allan has gained well-deserved recognition as an amazing baker, he is also an excellent cook with many years of culinary coaching under his belt. If you are looking for recipes written in a straightforward and clear approach, you will enjoy cooking from this book.

Home-cooked Meals: Favourite Asian Dishes and More is a celebration of the many cultures that influence the home kitchen in Singapore. The variety reflected in Allan's selection of recipes is undoubtedly inspired by his community of family and friends. It is a collection that will be treasured by novice and seasoned home cooks alike for its medley of flavours.

We hope that, with the help of this book, you will enjoy Allan's dishes the way we have, discover new favourites and share many home-cooked meals with your loved ones.

Sam & Forest Leong

Acknowledgements

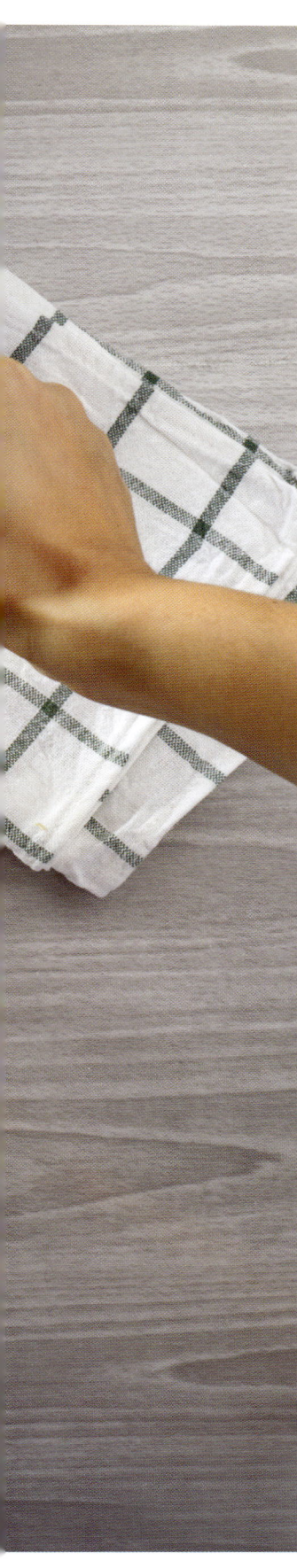

I would like to express my heartfelt appreciation to those who have helped in making this book a reality.

Many thanks to the team at Marshall Cavendish International (Asia), especially Lydia Leong, Lo Yi Min and Bernard Go, for this opportunity and their support in producing this book.

Ng Chai Soong brought the dishes to life in every shot with his artful photography and for that I am very thankful.

I am grateful to my business partner, Amy Ou, for her patience and support.

A massive thank you to Adrian Koh, Abigail Chay, Alice Shyu, Chen Yi Wei, Chiong Chee Yong, Ibrahim Ali, Jessie Phua, Josephine Martin, Lionel Chia, Lee Soon Teck, Ow Yong, Margaret Sng, Ng Hwee Hsien, Ng Hwee Leng, Puspa d/o N G Pillai, Serine Tan and Shuhada Bte Ridwan for having faith in me and helping me test each recipe numerous times.

A special thank you goes to my friend Karen Tan for her generous encouragement and support.

I would like to thank Philip Ang of Creation Venture Enterprise Pte Ltd for his generosity and kindness.

Finally, I am deeply thankful to my family and extended family for their constant encouragement and for keeping me sane while I worked on this book.

Introduction

The idea for this book was prompted by my nephew Songzhi when he sought advice from me on preparing a dish that I made at home often — sweet and sour prawns. At that time, he had just gone abroad to study and wanted to prepare his own meals. It occurred to me then that I hadn't written down my recipes for my family to refer to. Thus, I began compiling recipes for easy-to-make dishes that would remind Songzhi of home.

When I consider food that reminds me of home, I think of all the dishes I can enjoy in Singapore, including foods from different cultures. This collection also includes dishes that I've tried — whether prepared by friends or from a hawker stall or restaurant — which I would then recreate at home. I also share recipes for traditional dishes that were passed to me by my mother who was a great cook.

Students I meet in class often cite complex steps and ingredients that are difficult to obtain as reasons why they avoid cooking at home. I'd like to encourage more people to cook and enjoy a meal at home, so I've tried my best to use ingredients that are readily available in wet markets or supermarkets. I've also kept the steps straightforward, but feel free to experiment and make adjustments to suit your own palate. Cooking at home should be a playful experience; you'll get a good meal and lots of fun from the whole process.

The preparation of food is a multi-sensory engagement. While testing and tweaking the recipes for this book, I had the pleasure of taking in delightful aromas; like the warmth and sweetness of five-spice powder, and the bright citrusy notes of lemons; and tasting hot and fiery chillies, and countering the spiciness with the creamy and sour tang of yoghurt. I sincerely hope that you will have as much fun preparing these dishes as I had.

Happy cooking!

Allan Albert Teoh

SOUPS

Lotus Root Soup with Pork Ribs

Chicken Soup with Burdock Root and Mushrooms

Soto Ayam

Rasam

Sup Kambing

Lotus Root Soup with Pork Ribs

Serves 3

200 g lotus root
200 g pork ribs
2 litres water

80 g dried raw peanuts
6 dried scallops
2 dried cuttlefish, medium

6 dried red dates with seeds
Salt, to taste

1. Peel lotus root and slice into 1-cm thick pieces.
2. Bring a pot of water to a boil. Blanch pork ribs briefly in boiling water, drain and set aside.
3. In a pot over medium heat, place 2 litres water, lotus root, peanuts, scallops, cuttlefish and red dates. Bring to a boil and boil for about 1 hour.
4. Lower the heat, add pork ribs and simmer soup for another 1–2 hours until pork ribs are cooked through and tender.
5. Season with salt to taste before ladling into bowls. Serve hot.

Chicken Soup with Burdock Root and Mushrooms

Serves 4

8 dried Chinese mushrooms, soaked in 500 ml hot water for 20 minutes

2 litres water

1 burdock root (about 60 cm)

5 chicken wings

1/2 tsp salt

1. Drain mushrooms and squeeze to remove excess water. Reserve 200 ml soaking liquid.
2. Cut off mushroom stems and slice caps into halves.
3. Fill a large soup pot with 2 litres water.
4. Peel burdock root and cut diagonally into 1-cm thick chunks. Place cut burdock root immediately in soup pot to prevent browning.
5. Add mushrooms, soaking liquid and chicken wings, and bring to a boil over medium-low heat. Simmer for about 2 hours.
6. Season with salt before ladling into bowls. Serve hot.

Soto Ayam
Spiced Chicken Soup

Serves 5

2 large red onions, peeled

4 cloves garlic, peeled

3-cm knob old ginger, peeled

1 litre water

½ chicken (about 600 g)

5 Tbsp corn oil

1 stalk lemongrass (white portion only), crushed

3 cardamom pods

4 cloves

1 cinnamon stick

1 star anise

2 Tbsp *mee soto* mix, mixed with 1 Tbsp water to make a paste

Salt, to taste

CHILLI SAUCE

1–2 Tbsp dark soy sauce

6 bird's eye chillies (*cili padi*), sliced

2 Tbsp lime juice

1 Tbsp castor sugar

ACCOMPANIMENTS AND GARNISHING

500 g store-bought pressed rice cakes (*lontong*)

A handful of bean sprouts

Spring onions, as desired, chopped

Coriander leaves, as desired

Fried shallot crisps, as desired

1. Using a food processor, blend onions, garlic and ginger together until fine. Set aside.

2. In a large pot over medium-high heat, place water, chicken, oil, lemongrass, cardamom, cloves, cinnamon and star anise. Bring to a boil, then lower the heat.

3. Add onion mixture and *mee soto* paste. Boil until chicken is cooked through. Add salt to taste.

4. Remove chicken from pot and set aside to cool. Leave soup to boil for another 5 minutes before turning off the heat.

5. Debone cooled chicken and shred meat.

6. Prepare chilli sauce. Combine all ingredients in a bowl and mix well.

7. Prepare accompaniments. Cut pressed rice cakes into desired size and place in bowls. Parboil bean sprouts and add to bowls. Add shredded chicken and soup. Garnish with spring onions, coriander leaves and fried shallot crisps.

8. Serve with chilli sauce.

Rasam
Sour Tomato Soup

Serves 5

2 Tbsp tamarind (*asam*) paste, soaked in 500 ml warm water for 15 minutes

1/8 tsp ground turmeric

2 Tbsp black peppercorns

1/2 Tbsp cumin seeds

1/2 Tbsp mustard seeds

5 cloves garlic, left unpeeled

2 1/2 Tbsp corn oil

1 small onion, peeled and thinly sliced

5 dried red chillies, seeds removed

15 curry leaves

2 tomatoes, cut into chunks

250 ml water

1/2 tsp salt

1 sprig coriander leaves, roughly chopped

1. Strain tamarind mixture to remove pips and obtain juice. Stir ground turmeric into juice and set aside.

2. Using a spice grinder or mortar and pestle, grind or pound peppercorns, cumin seeds, mustard seeds and garlic until spices are fine but not powdery.

3. In a heavy-bottomed saucepan over medium-high heat, heat oil and fry onion for about 1 minute. Add chillies, curry leaves and spice mixture. Stir for another minute.

4. Add tomatoes and tamarind juice mixture. Bring to a boil, then lower the heat and simmer for 5–10 minutes.

5. When small bubbles form along the side of the pot, add 250 ml water and heat for 1 minute. Adjust the consistency of the soup with more water as desired. Season with salt.

6. Garnish with coriander leaves and serve hot. Rasam can be kept overnight for its flavours to develop further. Reheat and garnish before serving with basmati rice.

Sup Kambing
Spiced Mutton Soup

Serves 5

500 g mutton ribs

2 Tbsp black peppercorns, crushed

800 ml water

3 cloves garlic, peeled

3-cm knob old ginger, peeled

3 large red onions, peeled

4–5 Tbsp corn oil

1 cinnamon stick, broken into halves

2 star anise

3 cloves

2 cardamom pods

2 Tbsp spicy meat curry powder, mixed with 1 Tbsp water to make a paste

2 potatoes, peeled and quartered

50 ml evaporated milk

3 stalks celery, thinly sliced

Salt, to taste

Juice from $1/2$ lemon (optional)

100 g fried shallot crisps

3 sprigs coriander leaves, finely chopped

1. Place mutton ribs, peppercorns and water in a heavy-bottomed saucepan. Bring to a boil over medium-high heat. Boil for 30–40 minutes. Turn off the heat, drain mutton ribs and reserve 500 ml cooking liquid as stock. Set aside.

2. Using a food processor, blend garlic, ginger and 2 red onions together until fine. Set aside.

3. Slice the remaining red onion.

4. Heat oil in a frying pan over medium-high heat. Sauté sliced onion, cinnamon, star anise, cloves and cardamom. Add garlic mixture and stir-fry until aromatic. Add curry powder paste and fry until mixture is heated through.

5. Add reserved stock and simmer for 2–3 minutes. Add potatoes and cook for 20–25 minutes, until three-quarters cooked. A chopstick should pierce the potatoes easily, but the potatoes should still feel firm.

6. Add evaporated milk, celery and mutton ribs. Simmer soup for 10–15 minutes over low heat. Add salt to taste. For a more tangy flavour, stir in lemon juice.

7. Ladle into bowls and garnish with fried shallot crisps and coriander leaves. Serve hot with bread.

VEGETABLES

Acar

Cucumber Raita

Chap Chye

Stir-fried Ladies' Fingers

Spinach Curry

Sayur Lodeh

Crispy Vegetarian Yam Ring

Acar
Spicy Pickled Vegetables

Makes five 500-ml bottles

---

5 medium cucumbers, cored and cut into 3- to 4-cm strips

2½ tsp salt

260 ml white vinegar

1½ medium carrots, peeled and cut into 3- to 4-cm strips

125 g long beans, cut into 3- to 4-cm lengths

125 g cauliflower, cut into small florets

1 Tbsp tamarind (*asam*) paste, soaked in 120 ml water

60 ml corn oil

2 stalks lemongrass (white portion only), crushed

220 g yellow rock sugar

1 small pineapple, cored and cut into small triangles

120 g peanuts, roasted and coarsely ground

150 g sesame seeds, toasted until golden brown

1 torch ginger bud, finely shaved

REMPAH

16 dried red chillies, soaked in warm water, seeds removed

8 bird's eye chillies (*cili padi*)

6 green chillies

20 shallots, peeled

3-cm knob turmeric, peeled

3-cm knob galangal, peeled

---

1. Sprinkle cucumbers with salt. Mix well to coat and set aside. After 6–7 hours, squeeze cucumbers to remove juice. Spread on a tray and leave to dry, preferably in a sunny spot, for at least 24 hours.

2. Place vinegar, carrots, long beans and cauliflower in a medium pot. Bring to a boil and boil for 2–3 minutes. Drain vegetables and set aside.

3. Strain tamarind mixture to remove pips and obtain juice. Set aside.

4. Prepare *rempah*. Drain dried red chillies and combine with the remaining *rempah* ingredients in a food processor. Blend to form a smooth paste. You may also use a mortar and pestle instead.

5. Heat oil in a frying pan. Fry *rempah* with lemongrass until golden brown and aromatic. Add tamarind juice and sugar and cook until sugar is dissolved. Remove from heat and leave to cool completely.

6. In a large bowl, combine cooked *rempah* mixture, vegetables, pineapple, peanuts and sesame seeds. Mix well. Portion equally into bottles and top with torch ginger bud shavings. Cover bottles with lids and let sit for 2–3 days for flavours to develop before serving.

Cucumber Raita
Cucumber Yoghurt Salad

Serves 4

2 cucumbers, cored and cut into 1-cm cubes

1 Bombay onion or large red onion, peeled and diced

2 red chillies, seeds removed, diced

200 ml Indian yoghurt (*tairu*) or unsweetened yoghurt

$1/2$ tsp salt

1. In a large bowl, toss cucumbers, onion and chillies.
2. Add yoghurt and salt, and stir well to combine.
3. Refrigerate before serving chilled.

NOTE
To add a larger variety of vegetables, cut 8 cherry tomatoes into halves, and dice 1 stalk celery and 1 capsicum. Toss with cucumbers. Use 250 ml yoghurt and add more salt to taste.

Chap Chye
Mixed Vegetable Stew

Serves 5

---

3 Tbsp corn oil

20 g dried shrimps

3 cloves garlic, peeled and chopped

2 slices ginger, peeled

1½ Tbsp fermented soy bean paste (*tau cheo*)

150 g round cabbage, shredded

20 g baby corn, halved lengthwise

50 g carrot, stamped into flower shapes

5 dried wood ear (black) fungus, soaked in hot water to soften

5 dried Chinese mushrooms, soaked in hot water to soften, drained and sliced

10 boiled ginkgo nuts

10 snow peas

20 g dried lily buds, tips trimmed, knotted, soaked in hot water to soften and drained

300 ml water

1 tsp castor sugar + more as needed

1 tsp chicken seasoning powder + more as needed

½ tsp salt + more as needed

70 g glass noodles (*tang hoon*), soaked in water to soften and drained

5 dried bean curd sticks (*tau kee*)

---

1. Heat oil in a pot over medium-high heat. Add dried shrimps, garlic and ginger and fry for a few minutes. Stir in fermented soy bean paste and cook until fragrant.

2. Add cabbage, baby corn and carrot and stir-fry until the vegetables are softened.

3. Add dried wood ear fungus, mushrooms, ginkgo nuts, snow peas and dried lily buds. Stir well to mix.

4. Add enough water to cover the vegetables. You may not need to add all the water. Season with sugar, chicken seasoning powder and salt. Cover and let mixture simmer for 20–25 minutes over medium-low heat.

5. Add glass noodles and bean curd sticks and cook for another 5 minutes or until cooked through. Season to taste again.

6. Serve warm.

Stir-fried Ladies' Fingers

Serves 4

Corn oil, as needed
1/2 tsp cumin seeds
500 g ladies' fingers, tops trimmed, cut into 1-cm lengths
Salt, to taste
2 medium onions, peeled and diced
1 medium tomato, chopped
1/2 tsp ground coriander

1. Heat some oil in a wok over medium-high heat. Add cumin seeds and stir-fry for 20 seconds.
2. Add ladies' fingers and sauté for 3–4 minutes. Season with salt to taste.
3. Add onions and cook for 5 minutes until caramelised.
4. Add tomato and ground coriander. Cook for 1 minute.
5. Remove from heat and serve hot.

Spinach Curry

Serves 4

---

2 Tbsp ghee
½ tsp cumin seeds
2 bay leaves
½ tsp store-bought ginger-garlic paste
1 large onion, peeled and finely chopped
½ tsp chilli powder

½ tsp garam masala
¼ tsp ground turmeric
150 g spinach, chopped
4 Tbsp water
Salt, as needed
2 Tbsp Indian yoghurt (*tairu*) or unsweetened yoghurt

SPINACH PURÉE
125 ml water
250 g spinach, stems discarded
3 green chillies
5 cloves garlic, peeled
1.5-cm knob ginger, peeled

---

1. Prepare spinach purée. In a pot over medium-high heat, boil water and spinach leaves for 5 minutes until spinach leaves are soft. Drain spinach leaves and leave to cool.

2. Using a food processor, blend spinach leaves, green chillies, garlic and ginger together to form a smooth paste. Set aside.

3. Heat ghee in a large frying pan over medium-high heat. Add cumin seeds, bay leaves and ginger-garlic paste. Fry for 1 minute.

4. Add onion and fry until slightly brown. Add chilli powder, garam masala and ground turmeric and stir until well mixed before adding chopped spinach. Continue stirring until spinach is wilted.

5. Add spinach purée and cook for 5–10 minutes, stirring continuously.

6. Add water, adjusting amount for desired consistency. Lower the heat and simmer for 3–5 minutes. Season with salt to taste.

7. Stir in yoghurt and remove from heat.

8. Leave to cool slightly before serving.

Sayur Lodeh
Vegetable Coconut Curry

Serves 7

Corn oil, as needed

2 blocks yellow firm bean curd (*tauhu kuning*), each quartered diagonally

200 g tempeh, cut into 4-cm pieces

1 large red onion, peeled and cut into chunks

2 cloves garlic, peeled

1 stalk lemongrass (white portion only), thinly sliced

3-cm knob turmeric, peeled

3-cm knob old ginger, peeled

1-cm knob galangal, peeled

60 g dried shrimps, soaked in water to soften and drained

1 tsp salt + more as needed

500 ml coconut milk, combined with 100 ml water

1 medium carrot, peeled and sliced into 0.5-cm thick rounds

100 g long beans, cut into 1.5-cm lengths

1 yam bean (*sengkuang*), peeled and cut into even-sized strips

250 g cabbage, sliced into large rectangles

1 dried sour fruit slice (*asam gelugur / asam keping*)

SAMBAL PEDAS (OPTIONAL)

3 shallots, peeled and thinly sliced

5 bird's eye chillies (*cili padi*), thinly sliced

3 Tbsp sweet soy sauce (*kicap manis*)

1. Prepare *sambal pedas* if using. Combine all ingredients for *sambal pedas* in a bowl and mix well. Set aside.

2. Heat some oil in a frying pan over medium-high heat. Fry bean curd and tempeh until three-quarters cooked. Set aside.

3. Using a food processor, blend onion, garlic, lemongrass, turmeric, ginger, galangal, dried shrimps and salt together until fine. Set aside.

4. Heat 3–4 Tbsp oil in a frying pan over medium-high heat and fry onion mixture for about 5 minutes until oil separates from the paste.

5. Add coconut milk and simmer over low heat. Do not allow coconut milk to boil. Add carrot, long beans and yam bean, stirring occasionally. Cook until vegetables are tender. Add cabbage and dried sour fruit. Stir for 1 minute.

6. Add fried bean curd and tempeh and let mixture boil for 5–10 minutes. If necessary, adjust seasoning with more salt.

7. Remove from heat and serve immediately with *sambal pedas*. If desired, this dish can also be served with fried coconut flakes (*serunding*) and pressed rice cakes or rice.

Crispy Vegetarian Yam Ring

Serves 6–8

525 g yam

2½ Tbsp wheat starch + more if needed

2½ Tbsp hot water

1½ Tbsp castor sugar

¾ tsp salt

1 tsp five-spice powder

2 tsp sesame oil

A dash of ground white pepper

20 g rice vermicelli (*bee hoon*) (optional)

Coriander leaves, as desired

VEGETABLE FILLING

Corn oil, as needed

1 block firm bean curd (*tau kwa*), cut into bite-sized cubes

3 shallots, peeled and thinly sliced

4 dried Chinese mushrooms, soaked in hot water, stems discarded, cut into cubes

60 g celery, cut into cubes

60 g carrot, peeled and cut into cubes

100 g water chestnuts, peeled and cut into cubes

½ cucumber, cut into cubes

45 g dried wood ear (black) fungus, soaked in water for 15–20 minutes

30 g boiled ginkgo nuts

60 g cashew nuts, halved

SAUCE

4 Tbsp water

1 Tbsp tomato sauce

1 Tbsp chilli sauce

1¼ Tbsp white vinegar

2 Tbsp castor sugar

¾ Tbsp cornflour

1. Peel yam and cut into small pieces. Place in a steamer and cook over medium-high heat for 35–40 minutes. Remove cooked yam and mash into a smooth paste.

2. Mix wheat starch and hot water together. Add 1 1/2 Tbsp mixture to mashed yam. Mix well. Stir in sugar, salt, five-spice powder, sesame oil and pepper.

3. Knead mixture until it becomes a pliable dough that does not stick to your hands. If dough is too dry, add more wheat starch mixture. If dough is too sticky, add some wheat starch. Adjust with more seasoning to taste.

4. Mould yam dough into a ring of your desired size. Rest dough in freezer for 25–35 minutes until completely firm.

5. Prepare vegetable filling. Heat sufficient oil in a wok over medium-high heat. Fry bean curd for 5–10 minutes until golden brown. Remove bean curd from heat and set aside. Continue heating oil in the wok. Add shallots and mushrooms and sauté until fragrant. Add celery and carrots and stir for about 5 minutes. Mix in water chestnuts, cucumber, dried wood ear fungus and ginkgo nuts. Add fried bean curd and cashew nuts, mix well and transfer filling to a dish.

6. Prepare sauce. In the wok used to cook the filling, add all ingredients for the sauce and cook over medium-high heat until mixture thickens slightly. Turn off the heat, stir in filling and set aside.

7. In a wok over medium heat, add sufficient oil to submerge yam ring in. Test whether oil is ready by dipping a wooden chopstick into the hot oil. When small bubbles form around the chopstick, the oil is ready.

8. Add rice vermicelli and deep-fry until it floats to the surface. This should only take a few seconds. Transfer rice vermicelli quickly to drain on paper towels.

9. Place yam ring on a slotted ladle. Slowly submerge yam ring in oil. Deep-fry over medium heat for 10–15 minutes until light golden brown. Increase heat to high and deep-fry for 5 minutes until crispy. This will force out any oil trapped in the yam ring. Remove yam ring from heat carefully as it is very fragile.

10. Arrange fried rice vermicelli on serving plate and place yam ring on top. Pour filling into ring, garnish with coriander leaves and serve hot.

POULTRY & MEAT

Chicken Curry

Chicken and Chinese Mushroom Stew

Port Wine Chicken

Rosemary and Thyme Roast Chicken

Ayam Masak Merah

Pork Belly Slices

Braised Pork and Yam Slices

Fried Bakwan

Rendang Daging

Roasted Orange Lamb Chops

Mutton Keema

Satay Goreng Kambing

Chicken Curry

Serves 5

- 2.5-cm knob ginger, peeled
- 5 cloves garlic, peeled
- 5 shallots, peeled
- 5–6 Tbsp ghee
- 2 stalks curry leaves, leaves plucked, stems discarded
- 6 onions, peeled and sliced into rings
- 2 cinnamon sticks, broken into halves
- 10 cloves
- 10 cardamom pods
- 5 star anise
- 1/2 tsp ground turmeric
- 2 Tbsp meat curry powder
- 1 tsp ground cumin
- 1 Tbsp chilli powder
- 2 tsp garam masala
- 1/2 tsp ground bay leaf
- 5 large red chillies, cut lengthwise, seeds removed
- 5 medium tomatoes, puréed
- 1 kg chicken, chopped into small pieces
- Salt, to taste
- Ground black pepper, to taste
- 300 ml water + more as needed
- 100 ml coconut milk
- 2–3 sprigs coriander leaves, chopped

1. Using a food processor, blend ginger, garlic and shallots together until fine.
2. Heat ghee in a heavy-bottomed saucepan over medium heat. When ghee is heated, add curry leaves and onions. Sauté until onions are soft. Add cinnamon sticks, cloves, cardamom and star anise. Sauté for 1 minute. Add ginger mixture and continue stirring for 5–6 minutes or until aromatic.
3. Add ground turmeric, meat curry powder, ground cumin, chilli powder, garam masala and ground bay leaf and mix well. Stir in red chillies and tomato purée. Cook until oil separates from the paste.
4. Add chicken, turn the heat to medium-high and cook for 5–10 minutes. Season with salt and pepper to taste.
5. Add water and coconut milk and bring to a boil. Cover and simmer for 25–30 minutes or until chicken is cooked through.
6. Garnish with coriander leaves and serve hot with *roti prata* or rice.

Chicken and Chinese Mushroom Stew

Serves 5

3 Tbsp + 2 Tbsp oyster sauce

3 tsp sesame oil

1 Tbsp brandy or Shaoxing wine

Ground white pepper, as required

1 kg chicken, pat dry

2 Tbsp corn oil

3- to 4-cm knob old ginger, peeled and thinly sliced

4 cloves garlic, left unpeeled, lightly smashed

10 dried Chinese mushrooms, soaked in warm water for 30 minutes until soft, stems discarded

6 dried red dates with seeds

350 ml warm water + more as needed

1 1/2 tsp dark soy sauce

2 tsp castor sugar

Salt, to taste

2 spring onions, cut into 2-cm lengths

1. Combine 3 Tbsp oyster sauce, sesame oil, brandy or Shaoxing wine and a pinch of pepper to make a marinade.

2. Chop chicken into 16 pieces. Soak chicken in marinade for about 1 hour.

3. When chicken is ready to be cooked, heat corn oil in a wok or clay pot over medium heat.

4. Add ginger and garlic and stir until fragrant.

5. Add chicken and 2 Tbsp oyster sauce and stir well until chicken is cooked. Taste and adjust with an additional tablespoonful of oyster sauce if necessary.

6. Add mushrooms and red dates. Add 350 ml warm water, or just enough to cover the chicken, and bring to a boil.

7. Simmer stew for 25–30 minutes or until chicken is tender. If you find the stew too thick, add more warm water. If you find it too thin, thicken with a mixture of 1/2 tsp cornflour and 1 tsp water.

8. Season with pepper, dark soy sauce, sugar and salt.

9. Garnish with spring onions and serve warm.

Port Wine Chicken

Serves 5

1 kg chicken, pat dry, chopped into 15 pieces
2 litres water
1 cinnamon stick
5 cloves

50 g castor sugar
50 ml dark soy sauce
40 ml rice vinegar
Ground black pepper, to taste
Corn oil, as needed

10 shallots, peeled and sliced
125 ml port wine
7 cream crackers, finely pounded

1. In a large pot over medium-high heat, place chicken, water, cinnamon stick and cloves, and bring to a boil. When it comes to a boil, remove from heat. Drain chicken and retain 200 ml chicken stock. Set aside.

2. Combine sugar, dark soy sauce, rice vinegar and pepper in a large bowl.

3. Heat sufficient oil in a wok. When oil is hot enough, fry chicken until slightly brown. Remove from heat and set aside.

4. In the same wok, add more oil and fry shallots until slightly brown and fragrant. Add soy sauce mixture and chicken. Stir-fry for 5 minutes.

5. Add port wine and 150 ml chicken stock. For a thinner gravy, add more stock. Simmer chicken until tender, then gradually add cream crackers to thicken the gravy.

6. When crackers are well incorporated, remove from heat and serve hot.

Rosemary and Thyme Roast Chicken

Serves 4–6

2 spring chickens (about 700 g each)	1 stalk fresh rosemary, leaves plucked, stem discarded	1 large lemon
1 tsp black peppercorns, coarsely ground + more as needed	1 tsp mustard powder	4 Tbsp olive oil
2 tsp + 1 tsp salt	8 small potatoes	1 large onion, peeled and sliced
3 Tbsp Worcestershire sauce	1 bulb garlic, left unpeeled and smashed	3 medium carrots, peeled and cut into chunks
A handful of fresh thyme		4 stalks celery, cut into 5-cm lengths

1. Wash and pat dry chickens. Rub ground peppercorn and 2 tsp salt on the outside.

2. Coat the outside and cavity of chickens with Worcestershire sauce and massage well. Rub thyme and rosemary over the sauce, followed by mustard powder. If desired, massage chickens with more ground peppercorn. Refrigerate and leave to marinate for 1 hour.

3. Fill a large pot with some water and add 1 tsp salt. Bring to a boil over medium heat. Cut potatoes into halves and add to the pot with garlic and lemon. Cook for 15–20 minutes. Drain and leave to cool for 3 minutes. Set aside garlic and lemon.

4. Preheat oven to 200°C. Remove chickens from the refrigerator.

5. Cut lemon into quarters. Stuff lemon and garlic into chicken cavities. Truss (tie up) each chicken with kitchen string to make more compact, then with drizzle olive oil.

6. Arrange onion, carrots, celery and potatoes in a roasting pan. Place chickens breast-side up in pan and roast for 20 minutes. Reduce oven temperature to 190°C and roast for 25 minutes. Turn chickens over and roast for another 30 minutes.

7. Test if the chicken is done by cutting into it between the leg and breast. The juices should run clear and the meat should be firm but not rubbery. If it is not done, roast for a few more minutes and test again.

8. Remove from the oven. Retrieve and discard lemon. Remove garlic, squeeze the pulp from each clove and smear all over chickens. Serve warm with roasted vegetables.

Ayam Masak Merah
Spiced Tomato Chicken

Serves 4–5

7 tomatoes

1 large red onion, peeled and cut into chunks

2 cloves garlic, peeled

3-cm knob old ginger, peeled

5 Tbsp corn oil

1 cinnamon stick

2 cardamom pods

2 cloves

1 dried sour fruit slice (*asam gelugur / asam keping*)

410 g tomato paste

500 g chicken, cleaned and chopped into 12 pieces

1 tsp salt

1 tsp ground white pepper

1 tsp chicken seasoning powder

1. Using a food processor, purée 5 tomatoes. Cut the remaining 2 tomatoes into quarters. Set aside.
2. Using a food processor, blend onion, garlic and old ginger together until fine.
3. Heat oil in a heavy-bottomed saucepan over medium-high heat. Add onion mixture, cinnamon, cardamom, cloves and dried sour fruit. Sauté until fragrant.
4. Stir in tomato purée and tomato paste. Simmer for 2–3 minutes to cook tomatoes.
5. Add chicken and simmer for 10–15 minutes until chicken is cooked through.
6. Add chopped tomatoes, salt, pepper and chicken seasoning powder to taste. Simmer for 5 minutes to cook tomatoes.
7. Serve warm with rice.

Pork Belly Slices

Serves 5

PORK BELLY SLICES
500 g pork belly, blanched in hot water
$3/4$ tsp salt
2 litres water
2 Tbsp Shaoxing wine
10 cloves garlic, peeled
$1/2$ tsp black peppercorns

SOY CHILLI SAUCE
10 bird's eye chillies (*cili padi*)
2 red chillies
Juice from 8 limes
$1/4$ tsp salt
1 tsp castor sugar
2 Tbsp dark soy sauce

VINEGAR CHILLI SAUCE
2 bird's eye chillies (*cili padi*), thinly sliced
3 cloves garlic, peeled and finely chopped
$1/2$ tsp salt
2 Tbsp rice vinegar

1. Prepare pork belly slices. Rub pork belly with salt and marinate for 1.5–2 hours.
2. In a heavy-bottomed saucepan over medium-high heat, place water, Shaoxing wine, garlic and black peppercorns. Boil for 15–20 minutes.
3. Keep mixture at a rolling boil and add pork belly. Boil for about 15 minutes over high heat. Lower the heat to medium and cook for 45 minutes until cooked through.
4. Transfer pork belly to a colander and let it drip dry.
5. Prepare soy chilli sauce. Using a food processor, blend all ingredients except dark soy sauce until fine. Place dark soy sauce in a condiment dish, add blended mixture and stir to mix.
6. Prepare vinegar chilli sauce. Combine all ingredients in a bowl and stir well. Transfer to a condiment dish.
7. Cut pork belly into thin slices and serve with sauces.

Braised Pork and Yam Slices

Serves 5

400 g roast pork
450 g yam
Corn oil as needed
4 cloves garlic, peeled and chopped
1 tsp minced shallots

½ tsp minced ginger
3 star anise
1 cube red fermented bean curd, mashed
2 Tbsp Shaoxing wine
1 ½ tsp castor sugar

Ground white pepper, to taste
3 Tbsp water
Coriander leaves, chopped, as desired

1. Prepare a steamer.
2. Cut roast pork into 0.2- to 0.3-cm thick slices. Set aside.
3. Rinse yam and pat dry. On a dry chopping board, slice off yam skin. Cut yam into 0.2- to 0.3-cm thick rectangles. Do not let yam slices come into contact with water as they will become starchy, affecting the texture and taste of the dish.
4. Heat sufficient oil in a wok. Test whether oil is ready by dipping a wooden chopstick into the hot oil. When small bubbles form around the chopstick, the oil is ready.
5. Deep-fry yam slices until golden brown. Drain yam slices.
6. Sandwich a yam slice between 2 slices of roast pork and arrange on a plate. Repeat until pork and yam slices are used up. Cover with aluminium foil and steam over medium-high heat for about 1 hour. Transfer to a serving dish.
7. Heat some oil in a saucepan over medium heat. Sauté garlic, shallots, ginger and star anise until fragrant. Stir in red fermented bean curd, Shaoxing wine and sugar. Season with pepper to taste. If gravy is too thick, adjust by adding water a little at a time. Bring to a boil.
8. Remove gravy from heat and spoon over pork and yam.
9. Garnish with coriander leaves and serve hot with rice.

Fried Bakwan
Fried Pork Balls

Serves 6

1 kg minced lean pork

500 g prawns, shelled, deveined and finely cubed

6 dried Chinese mushrooms, soaked in salt water

8–10 water chestnuts, peeled

½ medium carrot, peeled

Corn oil, as needed

½ cucumber, sliced (optional)

1 tomato, sliced (optional)

Sweet chilli sauce, as desired (optional)

Mayonnaise, as desired (optional)

MARINADE

3 Tbsp light soy sauce

2 Tbsp sesame oil

2 Tbsp cornflour

¼ tsp salt

½ tsp ground white pepper

2 tsp castor sugar

1. Prepare marinade. Combine all ingredients in a bowl and mix well.
2. Place pork and prawns in a large mixing bowl. Add marinade and mix using your hands until combined. Wrap pork mixture with cling film and refrigerate for about 1 hour.
3. Cut off mushroom stems. Chop mushrooms, water chestnuts and carrot finely.
4. Remove pork mixture from the refrigerator and add mushrooms, water chestnuts and carrot. Mix until combined and wrap once more in cling film. Refrigerate for 2–3 hours or overnight.
5. Remove pork mixture from the refrigerator and knead to mix once more.
6. Form mixture into balls, about 20 g each. Using a slapping motion, lightly toss each ball from one hand to the other 5–6 times. This helps the meat to hold together better.
7. Heat sufficient oil in a heavy-bottomed saucepan or wok over medium-high heat. When oil is hot enough, fry balls until golden brown, turning them over from time to time to ensure even browning. Drain pork balls on paper towels.
8. Serve warm on a bed of sliced cucumbers and tomatoes. Offer sweet chilli sauce and mayonnaise on the side if desired.

Rendang Daging
Spicy Dry Beef Stew

Serves 6

350 g grated skinned coconut

8–9 Tbsp corn oil

750 ml coconut milk

500 g beef, cut into cubes

3 lime leaves, torn into small pieces

1 turmeric leaf, torn into small pieces

1 stalk lemongrass (white portion only), crushed

2 dried sour fruit slices (*asam gelugur / asam keping*)

Coriander leaves, as desired

Salt, to taste

REMPAH

2 large red onions, peeled and cut into chunks

3 cloves garlic, peeled

1 stalk lemongrass (white portion only), thinly sliced

3-cm knob old ginger, peeled

3-cm knob galangal, peeled

15 dried red chillies, soaked in hot water for 20 minutes and drained, seeds removed

5 red chillies

SLICED HERBS

3 lime leaves, thinly sliced

1 turmeric leaf, thinly sliced

1. In a medium saucepan over medium heat, sauté grated skinned coconut without any oil until golden brown and dry. Keep stirring to ensure coconut does not burn. Set aside.

2. Prepare *rempah*. Using a food processor, blend all ingredients together until fine.

3. Heat oil in a heavy-bottomed saucepan over medium-high heat. Add *rempah* and sauté until aromatic and oil separates from the paste. Add coconut milk and bring to a simmer, stirring often.

4. Add beef, lime leaves, turmeric leaf, lemongrass and dried sour fruit. Cover and simmer over medium-low heat for 25 minutes, stirring occasionally.

5. Add grated coconut, coriander leaves and sliced herbs. Reduce the heat to low. Stir frequently while simmering for 20–25 minutes until almost dry.

6. Add salt to taste and remove from heat.

7. Top with more coriander leaves as desired and serve warm.

Roasted Orange Lamb Chops

Serves 2

500 g lamb chops (about 4)
Unsalted butter, as needed
4 sprigs rosemary
1 orange, thinly sliced

MARINADE
1 orange, juiced and zested
4 Tbsp unsweetened yoghurt
2 stalks lemongrass (white portion only), bruised
2 tsp ground turmeric

1 Tbsp black peppercorns, crushed
2 Tbsp minced garlic
1/2 tsp salt
4 Tbsp honey
45 g unsalted butter, softened

1. Prepare marinade. Combine all ingredients in a bowl and give it a good stir.
2. Place lamb chops in a zip-lock bag and pour in marinade. Refrigerate to season overnight.
3. Preheat oven to 190°C.
4. Transfer lamb chops to a roasting pan and roast for 10 minutes. Baste with drippings and top each lamb chop with a small dollop of butter. Roast for a further 10–15 minutes or until desired doneness.
5. Remove from oven and garnish with rosemary and thinly sliced oranges. Serve warm.

Mutton Keema
Minced Mutton and Tomato Stew

Serves 5

½ tsp salt

1 Tbsp + 230 ml water

6 cloves garlic, peeled and minced

1 Tbsp ground coriander

1 Tbsp ground turmeric

1 Tbsp cumin seeds

7 red chillies, seeds removed, cut into thin strips

4 Tbsp ghee

2 large onions, peeled and sliced

5 green chillies, chopped

30 g ginger, peeled and julienned

3 tomatoes, peeled and chopped

400 g minced mutton, blanched in warm water

245 g Indian yoghurt (*tairu*) or unsweetened yoghurt

1 tsp garam masala

¼ tsp saffron, soaked in 1 Tbsp warm milk

20 roasted cashew nuts

Coriander leaves, as desired

1. Using a food processor, blend salt, 1 Tbsp water, garlic, ground coriander, ground turmeric, cumin seeds and red chillies together to form a fine paste. Set aside.

2. Heat ghee in pan over medium-high heat. Fry onions, green chillies, ginger and tomatoes until brown, and ghee begins to separate from mixture. Add spice paste and simmer for 4 minutes.

3. Add minced mutton and simmer for 4–5 minutes.

4. Add yoghurt and 230 ml water. Cook until mutton is done and gravy is thick.

5. Add garam masala, saffron mixture and cashew nuts. Cover and simmer mixture for 4–5 minutes.

6. Garnish with coriander leaves and serve hot.

Satay Goreng Kambing
Fried Mutton Satay

Serves 6

500 g mutton

4 Tbsp corn oil

MEAT MARINADE

2½ Tbsp cumin seeds

2½ Tbsp black cumin seeds (*kala jeera*)

1 Tbsp black peppercorns

2½ Tbsp coriander seeds

2 Tbsp dark soy sauce

2 Tbsp light soy sauce

1 Tbsp oyster sauce

1 tsp salt

2 tsp ground white pepper

PEANUT SAUCE

10 dried red chillies, soaked in warm water

2 large red onions, peeled and cut into chunks

3 cloves garlic, peeled

3-cm knob old ginger, peeled

3-cm knob turmeric, peeled

4 Tbsp corn oil

70 g tamarind (*asam*) paste, soaked in 350 ml warm water and strained to obtain 320 ml tamarind juice

6 Tbsp castor sugar

250 g raw peanuts, roasted, skins removed and coarsely chopped

1. Wash mutton and cut into bite-sized pieces. Set aside.

2. Prepare meat marinade. In a heavy-bottomed saucepan over medium-high heat, toast cumin and black cumin seeds, peppercorns and coriander seeds until fragrant. Place in a spice grinder and grind until fine.

3. In a large mixing bowl, combine dark and light soy sauces, oyster sauce, salt, white pepper and ground spices and mix well. Add mutton, mix and marinate overnight in the refrigerator.

4. To cook mutton, heat oil in a heavy-bottomed pan over medium-high heat. Fry mutton for 10–15 minutes until cooked. Set aside.

5. Prepare peanut sauce. Drain dried red chillies and place in a food processor. Add onions, garlic, ginger and turmeric. Blend together until fine and set aside.

6. Heat oil in a heavy-bottomed saucepan over medium-high heat. Add chilli mixture and stir-fry until aromatic. Add tamarind juice and sugar, and cook for 5–10 minutes. Add peanuts and cook for 5 minutes.

7. Serve mutton with peanut sauce on the side. Alternatively, pour peanut sauce over mutton before serving.

NOTE
Beef or chicken can be substituted for mutton. If substituting with chicken, use chicken breast and increase the quantity to 700 g.

SEAFOOD

Sweet and Sour Prawns

Gulai Kunyit Udang

Prawn Fritters

Asam Fish

Fish Head Curry

Baked Salmon with Herbs and Honey Butter

Steamed Flower Crabs in Bean Paste

Stir-fried Squid with Chinese Chives

Sotong Masak Hitam

Sweet and Sour Prawns

Serves 4

1 1/2 Tbsp Shaoxing wine

1 Tbsp light soy sauce

1 egg white

1 Tbsp + 2 Tbsp water

1 Tbsp custard powder

600 g medium prawns, peeled and deveined, leaving tails intact

1 Tbsp white vinegar

1/2 Tbsp castor sugar

1 medium cucumber, cored, cut into thirds, then into thin strips

1/2 medium onion, peeled

1/2 red capsicum, seeds and core removed

1/2 yellow capsicum, seeds and core removed

1/2 green capsicum, seeds and core removed

1/2 medium tomato

1 small pineapple, peeled

Corn oil, as needed

SAUCE

1 Tbsp custard powder

150 ml water

1 Tbsp white vinegar

2 1/2 Tbsp tomato sauce

1/2 tsp chicken seasoning powder

2 Tbsp castor sugar

2 tsp light soy sauce

1 1/2 tsp sesame oil

1 1/2 Tbsp corn oil

4 cloves garlic, peeled and minced

1. Combine Shaoxing wine, soy sauce, egg white and 1 Tbsp water in a large bowl. Stir in custard powder. Add prawns and marinate for 2 hours.

2. Combine white vinegar, 2 Tbsp water and sugar in a bowl. Add cucumber and marinate for 2 hours. Drain cucumber and leave on paper towels to dry.

3. Cut onion, capsicums, tomato and pineapple into bite-sized pieces. Set aside.

4. To cook prawns, heat sufficient oil in a frying pan over medium heat. Add prawns and sauté for 1–2 minutes until prawns are a light orange. Place on paper towels to drain off excess oil. Set aside.

5. In the same frying pan, add 1 1/2 Tbsp oil and sauté onion for 30 seconds. Add capsicums, cucumber, tomato and pineapple. Stir-fry for 1–2 minutes. Set aside.

6. Prepare sauce. Combine custard powder and water in a bowl. Stir until custard powder is dissolved before adding the remaining ingredients except corn oil and garlic.

7. Heat corn oil in a saucepan over medium-low heat. When oil is hot enough, sauté garlic for 30 seconds. Add custard mixture and simmer for 2 minutes.

8. Add vegetables and stir for about 1 minute before adding prawns. Remove from heat and toss to coat prawns and vegetables with sauce. Serve hot.

Gulai Kunyit Udang
Turmeric Curry Prawns

Serves 6

4 knobs turmeric, each about 5-cm, peeled
5 cloves garlic, peeled
15 shallots, peeled
6 candlenuts

125 ml corn oil
5 stalks lemongrass (white portion only), lightly crushed
Salt, to taste
Castor sugar, to taste

18 large prawns
180 ml coconut milk
Water, as needed
1 tomato, diced
2 large red chillies, sliced

1. Using a food processor, blend turmeric, garlic, shallots and candlenuts together to form a paste.
2. Heat oil in a wok over medium-high heat. Add paste and lemongrass and cook for about 20 minutes until fragrant.
3. Add salt and sugar to taste.
4. Add prawns and coconut milk. Dilute with some water if curry is too thick. Cook for 5–10 minutes until prawns are done.
5. Add tomato and stir to combine. Remove from heat.
6. Garnish with red chillies and serve warm.

Prawn Fritters

Serves 4

500 g large prawns, peeled and deveined, leaving tails intact
1/8 tsp salt
1/8 tsp ground white pepper
Corn oil as needed

BATTER
200 g self-raising flour
A pinch of salt
120–140 ml cold water

1. Season prawns with salt and pepper. Refrigerate uncovered for about 1 hour until prawns are dry to the touch. Dab with paper towels to absorb any excess moisture. The prawns must be dry so that the batter will stick.

2. Prepare batter. Sift flour and salt into a bowl. Add water gradually and whisk until well mixed. You may not need to add all the water. The batter should be thick enough to coat the prawns. If batter is too thin, adjust with more flour a little at a time.

3. Heat sufficient oil in a wok. While oil is heating, dip prawns into batter, making sure each prawn is evenly coated.

4. Test whether oil is ready by dipping a wooden chopstick into the hot oil. When small bubbles form around the chopstick, the oil is ready.

5. Lower a few prawns into the oil and reduce heat to medium. Do not attempt to fry too many prawns at a time as this will lower the temperature of the oil. Deep-fry until golden brown and when there are almost no bubbles around prawn fritters. Increase heat to high before removing prawn fritters and draining on paper towels. Repeat until all prawns are fried.

6. Leave to cool slightly before serving.

Asam Fish
Sour and Spicy Fish Stew

Serves 4

4 medium tomatoes

3 1/2 Tbsp corn oil

6 ladies' fingers, cut into halves

1 dried *asam* skin (*asam kandis* / *asam kulit*)

1 large onion, peeled and cut into quarters

600 g mackerel

Coriander leaves, as desired

REMPAH

12 dried red chillies, soaked in hot water for 15 minutes, seeds removed

5 red chillies, seeds removed

3 bird's eye chillies (*cili padi*), seeds removed

6 cloves garlic, peeled

2-cm knob ginger, peeled

2-cm knob galangal, peeled

1-cm knob turmeric, peeled

3 candlenuts

1 tsp dried shrimp paste (*belacan*)

ASAM SAUCE

3 1/2 Tbsp tamarind (*asam*) paste

600 ml water

1/2 tsp salt

1 Tbsp castor sugar

3 stalks lemongrass (white portion only), bruised

1. Place tomatoes in a pot and add enough boiling water to cover them. Cover pot and let sit for a few minutes before draining. Peel tomatoes and chop into quarters. Set aside.

2. Prepare *asam* sauce. Combine all ingredients in a pot over medium-high heat and bring to a boil. Simmer for about 20 minutes before straining sauce. Discard tamarind pips and return lemongrass to sauce. Set aside.

3. Prepare *rempah*. Drain dried red chillies and place in a food processor. Add the remaining ingredients for the *rempah* and blend to form a fine paste.

4. Heat oil in wok over medium-high heat. Add *rempah* and stir continuously until fragrant. Add *asam* sauce. Reduce heat to low and simmer for 10 minutes.

5. Add ladies' fingers, *asam* skin, onion and mackerel. Cook for about 10 minutes or until mackerel is cooked through.

6. Stir in tomatoes. Remove from heat, garnish with coriander leaves and serve hot.

Fish Head Curry

Serves 4

1 Tbsp sunflower oil

10 medium ladies' fingers, tops and ends trimmed

100 g tamarind (*asam*) paste, soaked in 380 ml water

2 medium onions, peeled, halved, then thinly sliced

3 tomatoes, cut into wedges

3 stalks curry leaves, leaves plucked, stems discarded

600 g red snapper fish head, cut into 4 sections

1 tsp chicken seasoning powder

Salt, to taste

200 ml coconut milk (optional)

2–3 sprigs coriander leaves, finely chopped

REMPAH

2.5-cm knob old ginger, peeled

4 red chillies, seeds removed

8 cloves garlic, peeled

4 shallots, peeled

Water, as needed

7 Tbsp sunflower oil

$^3/_4$ tsp fenugreek seeds

$^3/_4$ tsp fennel seeds

$2^1/_2$ Tbsp fish curry powder

$1^1/_2$ Tbsp garam masala

1 Tbsp chilli powder

$^1/_2$ tsp ground fennel

$^1/_2$ tsp ground cumin

A pinch of ground black pepper

A pinch of salt

1. Heat oil in a wok over medium heat. Add ladies' fingers and stir-fry for 1–2 minutes to prevent them from becoming slimy. Remove from heat and set aside.

2. Strain tamarind mixture to remove pips and obtain tamarind juice.

3. Prepare *rempah*. Using a food processor, blend ginger, chillies, garlic and shallots with a little water to form a fine paste.

4. Heat oil in a wok over medium heat. Add paste, the remaining *rempah* ingredients and 2 Tbsp tamarind juice. Stir-fry until aromatic and oil separates from the paste.

5. Lower the heat, add onions and fry until tender. Add tomatoes, curry leaves and the remaining tamarind juice. Boil mixture for 10–15 minutes until the gravy is reduced slightly.

6. Add fish head and simmer for 7–8 minutes until more of the gravy is evaporated.

7. Turn fish over and gently stir in ladies' fingers and chicken seasoning powder. Simmer for 7–8 minutes before adding salt to taste. Add coconut milk, if using, and bring to a boil.

8. Remove from heat and leave for at least 20–25 minutes to allow fish to soak up the flavours. Garnish with coriander leaves and serve hot with rice.

Baked Salmon with Herbs and Honey Butter

Serves 4

4 Tbsp unsalted butter, softened

3 Tbsp honey

4 Tbsp mixed herbs

1/2 tsp salt

4 salmon fillets

1. Preheat oven to 170°C. Line a baking tray with aluminium foil and grease foil.
2. Combine butter, honey, mixed herbs and salt in a mixing bowl and mix well.
3. Coat salmon generously with herb mixture.
4. Arrange salmon skin-side down on prepared baking tray. Let sit for about 30 minutes before baking for 15–20 minutes.
5. Serve hot.

Steamed Flower Crabs in Bean Paste

Serves 4

4 flower crabs	2 Tbsp corn oil
10 cloves garlic, peeled	350 ml water
1 red chilli	1 egg, lightly beaten
1½ Tbsp fermented soy bean paste (*tau cheo*)	

1. Prepare crabs by removing the hard shells and spongy gills. Chop crabs into halves. Wash and pat dry before setting aside.

2. Using a food processor, blend garlic and chilli together until fine. Add fermented soy bean paste and process until combined.

3. Heat oil in a wok over medium-high heat. Add blended paste and stir-fry until fragrant.

4. Add crabs and stir to coat evenly with paste.

5. Add water and bring to a boil. When water starts to boil, cover wok and simmer crabs for 10–15 minutes until cooked through.

6. Stir egg into sauce and mix well.

7. Transfer to a serving plate and serve hot with rice.

Stir-fried Squid with Chinese Chives

Serves 3

2 medium squid
1 1/2 Tbsp light soy sauce
1 tsp sesame oil
1/2 tsp ground white pepper
1 tsp cornflour
30 ml water

2 Tbsp corn oil
3 cloves garlic, peeled and minced
80 g Chinese chives, cut into 1-to 2-cm lengths
Salt, to taste

1. Clean squid and discard the innards.
2. Cut open squid tube and lightly score the inside surface of each squid in a criss-cross pattern using a knife. Slice squid into bite-sized pieces.
3. Combine squid with soy sauce, sesame oil and pepper in a bowl. Marinate for 1.5–2 hours.
4. Mix cornflour and water together. Set aside.
5. Heat corn oil in a wok over medium-high heat. Add garlic and stir-fry until slightly brown.
6. Add chives and stir-fry for 1 minute. Add squid and stir well. Season with salt to taste.
7. Add cornflour mixture and bring the gravy to a boil.
8. As squid overcooks easily, remove from heat once the squid curls up. Serve hot.

Sotong Masak Hitam
Squid in Black Ink

Serves 5

500 g squid

3–4 Tbsp corn oil

2 medium red onions, peeled and thinly sliced

3 cloves garlic, peeled and minced

3-cm knob old ginger, peeled and minced

2 stalks lemongrass (white portion only), sliced

3 lime leaves, torn into halves

3 red chillies, sliced

2 green chillies, halved lengthwise and seeds removed

Water as needed

1/2 tsp salt

1/2 tsp ground white pepper

1/4 tsp castor sugar

1. Clean squid and discard the innards. Reserve 4–5 squid ink sacs, which are small, tear-shaped silvery pouches. Break ink sacs over a bowl, collect ink and set aside.

2. Slice squid into 1-cm thick rings.

3. Heat oil in a frying pan over medium-high heat and sauté onion and garlic until aromatic. Add ginger, lemongrass and lime leaves and cook for 2 minutes.

4. Add red and green chillies and cook for 1 minute. Push mixture towards the sides of the pan to make a well before adding squid ink. Stir quickly to mix and add a little water if mixture is thick.

5. Add squid, salt, pepper and sugar and simmer for 1–2 minutes. Be careful not to overcook the squid.

6. Once squid is cooked through, remove from heat and serve hot.

NOTE
Be careful when breaking the ink sacs as the process can be quite messy. Ink stains on clothing can be difficult to remove.

RICE & NOODLES

- Nasi Ulam
- Baked Rice with Prawns
- Luncheon Meat Fried Rice
- Abalone Porridge
- White Bee Hoon
- Kampong Fried Noodles

Nasi Ulam
Mixed Herb Rice

Serves 6

400 g basmati rice, rinsed and soaked for 30 minutes
200 ml water
500 ml coconut milk
6 pandan leaves, torn into halves
2 stalks lemongrass (white portion only), crushed
60 g dried shrimps
60 g dried salted fish
Corn oil, as needed

½ turmeric leaf
15 mint leaves
15 basil leaves
15 polygonum (*laksa*) leaves
1 torch ginger bud
3–4 bird's eye chilli (*cili padi*), seeds removed, sliced
1 banana leaf

SAMBAL (OPTIONAL)
30 g shallots, peeled
30 g garlic, peeled
20 g old ginger, peeled
20 g red chillies, seeds removed
1 stalk lemongrass (white portion only)
1 Tbsp dried shrimps
1 Tbsp chilli paste
Corn oil, as needed
1 tsp chicken seasoning powder
1 tsp castor sugar

1. Drain rice and place in a rice cooker. Add water, coconut milk, pandan leaves and lemongrass. Cook rice using the regular rice setting. Discard pandan leaves and lemongrass when rice is cooked.

2. In a dry pan, toast dried shrimps without oil until crisp. Set aside.

3. Chop salted fish into small slivers. Heat some oil in a frying pan and fry fish until fragrant. Drain on paper towels.

4. Slice turmeric, mint, basil and polygonum leaves thinly. Slice tender portion of torch ginger bud and discard the rest.

5. In a large mixing bowl, place rice, sliced herbs, salted fish, dried shrimps and bird's eye chillies. Toss well. Line a serving plate with banana leaf and place rice in a mound in the centre. Serve with sambal on the side, if desired.

6. To prepare sambal, use a food processor to blend shallots, garlic, ginger, red chillies, lemongrass, dried shrimps and chilli paste together to form a paste.

7. Heat oil in a wok over medium heat and fry spice paste until fragrant. Stir in chicken seasoning powder and sugar. Remove and set aside to cool before serving.

Baked Rice with Prawns

Serves 4

140 g medium prawns, peeled, deveined and sliced into halves

1/8 tsp salt + more as needed

1/8 tsp ground black pepper + more as needed

1/2 tsp + 1/2 tsp Italian mixed herbs

2 Tbsp corn oil + more as needed

2 eggs, beaten

2 tsp minced garlic

4 Tbsp unsalted butter

2 Tbsp minced white onion

120 g frozen mixed vegetables

10 button mushrooms, sliced

240 g cooked long grain rice

120 g mozzarella cheese, grated

1. Season prawns with salt, pepper and 1/2 tsp Italian mixed herbs. Set aside for 1 hour.
2. Preheat oven to 180°C. Prepare four single-serving casserole dishes.
3. Heat oil in a wok over medium heat and fry eggs into an omelette. Remove omelette from heat and leave to cool. Cut cooled omelette into strips and set aside.
4. Add a little more oil into the wok and sauté garlic. Add prawns and fry until cooked. Set aside.
5. Heat a wok over medium heat and add butter. Add onion, mixed vegetables and mushrooms. Stir-fry for about 5 minutes.
6. Add rice and stir-fry until thoroughly mixed. Add omelette strips and mix well. Season with 1/2 tsp Italian mixed herbs, salt and pepper to taste.
7. Transfer rice to prepared casserole dishes. Cover with prawns and top with cheese.
8. Bake for 15–20 minutes until cheese is golden brown. Serve hot.

Luncheon Meat Fried Rice

Serves 5

1 1/2 Tbsp corn oil
1/2 Tbsp minced ginger
100 g luncheon meat, cut into small cubes
2 medium eggs, lightly beaten

400 g cooked long grain rice, prepared the day before and chilled overnight
8 French beans, chopped into 0.5-cm pieces
1 Tbsp light soy sauce
1 tsp ground white pepper

1. Heat oil in a wok over medium-high heat. When oil is hot, lower the heat to low and add ginger. Stir-fry until fragrant.
2. Add luncheon meat, increase the heat to medium and stir-fry for 1 minute.
3. Add eggs and continue to stir-fry for 30 seconds.
4. Add rice, increase the heat to high and fry for 5 minutes. Press the back of the spatula against any rice lumps to separate them.
5. Lower the heat to medium and add French beans, soy sauce and pepper. Fry for 1–2 minutes or until French beans are tender.
6. Transfer to a serving plate and serve hot.

Abalone Porridge

Serves 4

1 chicken breast
2 chicken carcasses
2.5 litres water
10 dried oysters
10 dried scallops
200 g long grain rice

Ground white pepper, to taste
1 Tbsp chicken seasoning powder
8 abalones (total about 150 g), cut into thin strips or leave whole, if desired

GARNISHING
A few stalks of spring onions, finely chopped
2–3 sprigs coriander, finely chopped
2 Tbsp fried shallot crisps

1. In a large pot over medium-high heat, bring chicken breast, chicken carcasses and water to a boil. Boil for 1.5 hours.
2. Remove chicken breast and leave to cool. Keep stock on the boil for another 30 minutes. Shred cooled chicken breast and set aside. Strain chicken stock and discard carcasses.
3. Return chicken stock to the pot. Add dried oysters and dried scallops and boil over medium-high heat for about 40 minutes until they are softened. Remove oysters and scallops and cut them into small strips. Set aside.
4. Add rice to chicken stock and boil for 30–40 minutes on high heat until rice is tender. Keep stirring to prevent porridge from sticking to the sides and bottom of the pot. Stir in oysters and scallops. Season with pepper and chicken seasoning powder. Add shredded chicken and stir to mix.
5. Remove from heat, add abalone and mix well.
6. Garnish with spring onions, coriander and fried shallot crisps. Serve hot.

White Bee Hoon
Braised Seafood Vermicelli

Serves 4

300 g medium prawns
1 litre water
1 1/2 tsp + 1 tsp salt
200 g pork belly, thinly sliced
200 g squid
2 Tbsp corn oil

4–5 cloves garlic, finely chopped
2 eggs, lightly beaten
60 g choy sum, cut into 4-cm lengths
2 Tbsp fish sauce
1/2 tsp ground white pepper

200 g rice vermicelli (*bee hoon*), soaked in water for 10 minutes and drained
100 g bean sprouts, tails removed
100 ml Chinese white rice wine
2–3 sprigs coriander, chopped into 1-cm lengths

1. Remove and clean prawn heads. Set aside for making stock. Peel and devein prawns, keeping tails intact. Set aside prawn shells for making stock.

2. In a large pot over medium heat, add water, prawn heads, prawn shells and 1 1/2 tsp salt to make stock. Bring to a boil and boil for 15 minutes.

3. Meanwhile, rinse pork slices with hot water and add to stock. Cook for 10 minutes, then remove pork slices and set aside.

4. Remove stock from heat and set aside.

5. Clean squid. Discard the innards and head. Slice into rings and set aside.

6. Heat oil in a wok over medium-high heat. Stir lightly to coat sides of the wok with oil. Add garlic and stir lightly.

7. Add half the eggs and stir until cooked before adding choy sum. Stir well. Add pork slices and 300 ml stock, and bring to a boil. Season with fish sauce, pepper and 1 tsp salt. Add the remaining portion of eggs and stir to incorporate.

8. Add rice vermicelli and stir to mix. Add more stock if mixture is dry or if you prefer a more soupy dish. Add prawns, squid, bean sprouts and rice wine. Stir to mix.

9. Cover and simmer for 1 minute to cook prawns and squid and allow rice vermicelli to absorb stock. Remove from heat and garnish with coriander. Serve hot.

NOTE
If desired, squeeze some lime juice over dish before serving. This dish can be accompanied by a dipping sauce of minced ginger, sliced chillies and apple cider vinegar.

Kampong Fried Noodles

Serves 5

1 large red onion, peeled and cut into chunks

1 clove garlic, peeled

10 dried red chillies, soaked with hot water for 20 minutes and drained

3 Tbsp corn oil

1 Tbsp sweet soy sauce (*kicap manis*)

1 medium egg, lightly beaten

500 g yellow noodles

1 tsp salt

1 tsp ground white pepper

200 g baby pak choi, ends trimmed, cut into small pieces

50 g bean sprouts, tails removed

OMELETTE STRIPS

2 Tbsp corn oil

2 medium eggs, beaten

GARNISHING

Sliced cucumbers, as desired

Sliced red chillies, as desired

1. Prepare omelette strips. Heat oil in a wok over medium heat and fry eggs into an omelette. Remove from heat and leave to cool. Cut cooled omelette into strips and set aside.

2. Using a food processor, blend onion, garlic and dried red chillies until fine.

3. Heat oil in a heavy-bottomed saucepan over medium-high heat and fry onion mixture until fragrant.

4. Add sweet soy sauce and egg and stir well to incorporate.

5. Add yellow noodles and mix well. Season with salt and pepper. Add baby pak choi and bean sprouts. Stir-fry for 2–3 minutes.

6. Remove from heat and garnish with cucumbers, red chillies and omelette strips. Serve hot.

DESSERTS

Green Bean Soup with Sago, Sweet Potato and Coconut Milk

Glutinous Rice Balls in Osmanthus Ginger Syrup

White Chocolate Blueberry Tart

Pulut Tai Tai

Rose Coconut Ladu

Gendang Kasturi

Green Bean Soup with Sago, Sweet Potato and Coconut Milk

Serves 6

60 g dried sago pearls
300 g sweet potatoes
1 Tbsp + 2 Tbsp castor sugar
90 g green beans, rinsed and drained
1.25 litres + 250 ml water
4–5 pandan leaves, cut into sections and torn into halves
100 g palm sugar (*gula melaka*)
180 ml coconut milk

1. Fill a medium pot with some water and bring to a boil over medium heat. When water boils, add sago pearls and simmer for 10 minutes, stirring occasionally to prevent sago pearls from clumping.

2. Remove pot from heat and cover for 5–10 minutes. When sago pearls are completely translucent, they are fully cooked. Drain in a mesh strainer and rinse with running water to remove any residual starch. Place in a bowl and fill with enough water to cover sago pearls. Set aside.

3. Peel sweet potatoes and cut into large cubes. Sprinkle with 1 Tbsp castor sugar and steam in a steamer over medium-high heat for 10–15 minutes until soft. Set aside to cool.

4. Place green beans, 1.25 litres water and pandan leaves in a large pot and bring to a boil. Boil for about 25 minutes.

5. Meanwhile, combine palm sugar and 250 ml water in a small pot. Bring to a boil and stir continuously until palm sugar melts. Remove from heat and strain to remove any sediment.

6. When green beans are cooked and softened, add sago pearls and 2 Tbsp castor sugar. Stir for 3–4 minutes before adding palm sugar syrup and coconut milk.

7. Add sweet potatoes, stir well and remove from heat. Serve warm.

Glutinous Rice Balls in Osmanthus Ginger Syrup

Serves 8

GLUTINOUS RICE BALLS

280 g glutinous rice flour

1 Tbsp tapioca flour

150 ml + 80 ml water

Food colouring paste, as desired

OSMANTHUS GINGER SYRUP

10-cm knob old ginger, peeled

2 litres water

4½ Tbsp dried osmanthus flowers

240 g rock sugar

1. Prepare glutinous rice balls. In a large mixing bowl, sift glutinous rice flour and tapioca flour together 3 times.

2. Bring 150 ml water to a rolling boil and add to flour mixture. Use a wooden spoon to mix well. Add 80 ml water gradually and, using your hands, knead until a smooth dough forms. If dough is too wet, adjust with more glutinous rice flour a tablespoonful at a time. If dough is too dry, adjust with more water a teaspoonful at a time. Knead until dough is soft but does not stick to your hand. Let dough rest at room temperature for 5–10 minutes.

3. Divide dough into portions, one for each food colouring used. Add a different food colouring to each portion and knead until the colour is even. Roll each portion into a log. Cut into small rounds, about 6–7 g each, and roll them into balls. Set aside.

4. Bring a pot of water to a boil over medium-high heat. When the water is at a rolling boil, lower glutinous rice balls into it. To prevent overcrowding, cook rice balls in batches. Keep pushing rice balls around the pot to prevent them from clumping. Boil for 1 minute or until rice balls float to the surface. Drain rice balls and place in a bowl of cold water to cool.

5. Prepare osmanthus ginger syrup. Grate ginger and place in a mesh strainer over a bowl. With a spoon, press ginger against the strainer to extract about 6½ tsp ginger juice. Set aside.

6. Place water in a pot over medium-high heat and bring to a boil. When water is boiling, add osmanthus and simmer for 15 minutes. Strain to remove osmanthus and set osmanthus aside.

7. Lower the heat to medium and add sugar to pot. Boil for 15 minutes until sugar is dissolved. Increase the heat to high and boil for 5 minutes. Turn off the heat and add ginger juice. Sprinkle osmanthus into the syrup as desired.

8. To serve, place rice balls into bowls. Ladle syrup into bowls and serve warm.

White Chocolate Blueberry Tart

Makes one 23-cm round tart

TART BASE
220 g all-purpose (plain) flour
2 Tbsp ground almonds
120 g unsalted butter, at room temperature
80 g icing sugar, sifted
1 small egg

FILLING
100 g white chocolate couverture buttons
60 ml whipping cream
15 g unsalted butter, softened
135 g mascarpone cheese, at room temperature
135 g cream cheese, at room temperature
50 g castor sugar
1 medium egg yolk

GARNISH
315 g blueberries, pat dry

1. Prepare tart base. Grease a 23-cm round fluted tart pan. Sift flour 3 times and combine with ground almonds. Mix well and set aside.

2. Using an electric mixer with a paddle attachment, cream butter and icing sugar at medium-high speed for 2–3 minutes until evenly mixed. Add egg and beat well to incorporate. Beat in flour mixture until a pliable dough forms.

3. On a lightly floured surface, roll dough into a large round about 0.5-cm thick. Line tart pan with dough and chill in the refrigerator for 1 hour.

4. Preheat oven to 180°C. Bake chilled tart base for about 15 minutes or until golden. Place pan on a wire rack and leave to cool completely before placing in the freezer. Keep oven heated at 180°C.

5. Prepare filling. Place white chocolate in a large bowl. Set aside.

6. In a heavy-bottomed saucepan over medium heat, heat whipping cream for 2–3 minutes, but do not let it boil. Pour cream over white chocolate and let mixture sit until chocolate is melted. Stir in butter and set aside.

7. Using an electric mixer with a paddle attachment, beat mascarpone cheese, cream cheese and castor sugar together at medium speed for 1 minute. Add chocolate mixture and egg yolk. Mix well to incorporate.

8. Remove tart shell from the freezer and pour in filling. Bake for 10–15 minutes. Transfer to a wire rack to cool completely before refrigerating for 2 hours or until filling is firm.

9. Garnish tart with blueberries and serve.

Pulut Tai Tai
Glutinous Rice Cakes with Coconut Jam

Serves 10

CARAMELISED COCONUT JAM (KAYA)
100 g + 460 g castor sugar
1 Tbsp + 3 Tbsp hot water
500 ml coconut milk
10 medium eggs
8 pandan leaves, torn into halves

GLUTINOUS RICE
16 dried blue pea flowers (*bunga telang*)
2 Tbsp hot water
650 g glutinous rice, rinsed and soaked in water for 2.5 hours
50 ml + 160 ml coconut milk
230 ml water
1 tsp salt
4 pandan leaves, torn into halves
2 banana leaves, pat dry

1. Prepare caramelised coconut jam. Heat 100 g sugar in a saucepan over medium-low heat until sugar is melted. Add 1 Tbsp hot water and continue cooking until sugar is caramelised. Add 3 Tbsp hot water. Continue stirring to obtain a caramel coloured syrup.

2. Remove from heat and add 460 g sugar and coconut milk, stirring until the sugar is dissolved. Add eggs and beat in gently.

3. Strain mixture into a clean double boiling pot and add pandan leaves. Place pot in a larger pot filled with water. Cook over medium heat for about 2.5 hours, stirring constantly with a whisk. When mixture thickens and looks smooth, remove from heat. Discard pandan leaves. Set aside to cool.

4. Prepare glutinous rice. Using a mortar and pestle, lightly pound blue pea flowers. Mix with 2 Tbsp hot water and strain to obtain blue colouring. Set aside.

5. Prepare a steamer. Drain rice and place in a large heatproof bowl. In a separate bowl, combine 50 ml coconut milk with water. Stir in salt and pour mixture over rice. Mix well with a pair of chopsticks. Add pandan leaves and stir to mix. Place in steamer and steam rice over medium-high heat for 30 minutes.

6. Discard pandan leaves and fluff rice with chopsticks. Add 160 ml coconut milk, mix well and steam over medium-high heat for 15 minutes. Drizzle blue colouring over rice and steam for another 15 minutes. Remove from heat and fluff rice again.

7. Line a 20-cm square tray with a banana leaf and grease lightly. Transfer rice onto tray and press down firmly with the back of a spoon. Cover with the remaining banana leaf and weigh it down with a heavy object. Set aside for 2 hours until completely cooled.

8. Cut rice cake into slices using a plastic knife wrapped in cling film or an oiled serrated knife. Serve with caramelised coconut jam.

Rose Coconut Ladu
Sweet Coconut Balls

Makes 12 balls

---

130 g desiccated coconut

110 ml coconut milk + more as needed

A pinch of salt

60 g condensed milk

1 Tbsp rose water

2½ Tbsp rose syrup

1 Tbsp coconut oil + more as needed

⅛ tsp ground cinnamon

---

1. Heat a non-stick frying pan over medium-low heat. Fry desiccated coconut until warm, but do not let it brown. Remove from heat and set aside 30 g for the coating.

2. Leave remaining desiccated coconut in the frying pan. Add coconut milk, salt, condensed milk, rose water and rose syrup, stirring continuously until well mixed.

3. Add coconut oil and ground cinnamon and mix to combine. Place frying pan over low heat to warm mixture and stir for 1 minute. If mixture is too dry at this stage, adjust by adding more coconut milk a tablespoonful at a time.

4. Remove mixture from heat. Oil your hands with some coconut oil and knead mixture lightly.

5. Divide into 12 equal portions and roll into balls. Coat balls with the reserved desiccated coconut.

6. Serve. Ladu will keep for up to 1 week, stored in an airtight container in the refrigerator.

Gendang Kasturi
Green Bean Paste Fritters

Serves 6

220 ml water
150 g green beans
2 pandan leaves, knotted
100 g granulated sugar
2 Tbsp all-purpose (plain) flour

1 Tbsp tapioca flour
3 Tbsp grated skinned coconut
1/2 tsp camphor (*kapur*), mixed with 1 tsp water
1/2 tsp salt
1/2 tsp ground turmeric

Corn oil, as needed

BATTER
120 g rice flour
1 Tbsp cornflour
150 ml water + more as needed

1. In a large pot over medium-high heat, bring water, green beans and pandan leaves to a boil. Cook for 30 minutes or until green beans are soft and water is reduced.

2. Add sugar and boil for a further 10–15 minutes until sugar is dissolved. Remove from heat and transfer to a large mixing bowl. Set aside.

3. Sift all-purpose flour and tapioca flour together 3 times. Add flour mixture, grated skinned coconut, camphor, salt and ground turmeric to green bean mixture. Mix well and leave to cool.

4. Roll cooled mixture into small round balls, about 20 g each, then flatten into 2-cm thick patties. Set aside.

5. Prepare batter. Sift rice flour and cornflour together 3 times. Add water and stir well to obtain a batter that flows in a steady stream but is not watery. Adjust consistency of batter to your preference. To thin the batter, add more water a little at a time.

6. Heat sufficient oil in a heavy-bottomed saucepan over medium-high heat. Test whether oil is ready by dipping a wooden chopstick into the hot oil. When small bubbles form around the chopstick, the oil is ready. If you have a cooking thermometer, heat oil to 230°C.

7. Dip green bean patties into the batter. Place a patty onto a large ladle and lower into the oil. Repeat to add more patties and deep-fry until golden brown. Do not attempt to fry too many patties at a time as this will lower the temperature of the oil and result in soggy patties.

8. Drain on paper towels and serve warm.

Glossary

Bay Leaves
These fragrant leaves from the laurel tree are available fresh or dried. Commonly used in Malay and Indian cuisines, bay leaves are often simmered whole, but they can also be ground into powder and used as part of a spice mix. Whole leaves are used only to provide flavour and should not be eaten.

Burdock Root
The taproot of the burdock plant grows up to a metre long but is usually sold in shorter sections. The cream coloured flesh discolours quickly when exposed to air, so it is best to prepare burdock root just before cooking or soak cut pieces in water with some vinegar or salt.

Candlenuts
Known as *buah keras* in Malay, this small waxy nut is related to the macadamia nut. It is often used in Asian dishes as a thickener and texture enhancer. As raw candlenuts are mildly toxic, they should always be cooked before consumption. As they are high in oil content, candlenuts turn rancid easily, so use them as soon as possible and store in the refrigerator to maximise shelf life.

Cardamom Pods
This is a spice that exudes a sweet aroma when cooked. There are two varieties of cardamom: green cardamom, also known as true cardamom; and black cardamom, which is larger and has a blackish-brown shell. Although ground cardamom is available, it loses its flavour quickly in this form, thus it is best to purchase whole pods and grind them as needed.

Cinnamon
This spice comes from the inner bark of cinnamomum trees. It has a sweet aroma and imparts a woody and spicy flavour to many Asian dishes. Cinnamon is available as sticks and in powder form. Store in an airtight container and place in a cool and dry place to preserve flavour.

Coconut
The seed of the coconut palm tree is known for its versatility. Its flesh is available fresh or dried, or processed into coconut cream, milk and oil. These forms of coconut are frequently used in Malay and Indian dishes.

Cumin Seeds
These small, boat-shaped seeds come from the cumin plant, which belongs to the parsley family. It is a distinctively aromatic spice found in many spice mixes for Indian dishes. Store in an airtight container to preserve flavour.

Dried Chinese Mushrooms
Compared to the fresh ones, dried Chinese mushrooms have a more developed flavour. They may also be called shiitake mushrooms or black mushrooms. They must be soaked in hot water before using, and the soaking water, along with the tough mushroom stems, can provide a lot of flavour in stock or soups.

Dried Lily Buds
These are the unopened flowers of the day lily plant. They are brownish yellow in colour and have a strong woody and earthy aroma. Also known as golden needles or *huang hua*, they are used in many Chinese dishes, especially in stews and soups, as a flavour enhancer.

Dried Red Dates
With wrinkly red skin, red dates resemble the fruit of the date palm, but they come from a different plant. Also called jujubes, they are widely cultivated in China and used in Chinese herbal drinks and soups. Red dates add sweetness when added to dishes due to their high sugar content.

Dried Scallops
Dried scallops, or conpoy, are made by treating and drying fresh scallops. They are used in Chinese soups, stews and sauces to impart a sweet umami flavour. Dried scallops will keep for a long time if stored in an airtight container and refrigerated.

Dried Shrimp Paste
This fermented condiment is more commonly known as *belacan* and widely used in South East Asian cuisine. An essential ingredient in many curries and sauces, it is made by fermenting shrimp mixed with salt and pounded into a paste. It is usually sold in sun-dried blocks, but is also available as a wet paste.

Dried Sour Fruit Slices
Known as *asam gelugur* or *asam keping* in Malay, this is the fruit of the garcinia atroviridis tree that is native to South East Asia. It lends a sourness to many soups and curries due to its acidity. It is available as sun-dried slices, sometimes referred to as tamarind slices despite being unrelated to the tamarind fruit.

Fennel Seeds
These seeds have a liquorice-like flavour and aroma. This spice pairs well with fish dishes and is used extensively in Indian cooking. It is also an ingredient in the Chinese spice mix, five-spice powder.

Fenugreek Seeds
These yellowish brown seeds are almost retangular in shape. They have a smell reminiscent of maple syrup and a subtle bitter taste. This is a spice that is used frequently in Indian dishes and it is commonly added to chutneys, pickles and curries.

Galangal
The rhizome of a plant in the ginger family, galangal is also known as greater galangal or blue ginger, or *lengkuas* in Malay. It is native to South East Asia and is widely used in the region as a spice in dishes. It has a ginger-like spiciness and is added to curries, stews and soups. Cut into smaller pieces for blending in a food processor as galangal is quite hard.

Ginkgo Nuts
These nut-like seeds of the ginkgo biloba tree are used in Chinese and Japanese cuisines. They are usually sold pre-cooked in cans. As ginkgo nuts contain a toxin that cannot be destroyed by cooking, it is best to limit the amount of ginkgo nuts consumed.

Lemongrass
The stalk of the lemongrass plant has a citrusy flavour with a hint of ginger. To use for cooking, the outer layers are removed and the stem is bruised to release the flavours. Lemongrass is often added to curries and soups, and can also be used for brewing tea.

Lotus Root
The rhizome of the lotus plant can grow up to 1.2 metres and is usually sold in segments. It has a thin brownish-yellow skin and its flesh is a greyish cream colour. Lotus root is often used in stir-fried dishes to add crunchiness. It is also often used in soups and has a mildly sweet flavour.

Ladies' Fingers
This fuzzy seed pod and the plant it comes from are also known as okra or bhindi. As ladies' fingers produce a slimy liquid when cooked, they are often added to curries and stews as a thickener. They also taste great sliced and fried until crispy.

Peanuts
Peanuts are the edible seeds of a legume plant. Also known as groundnuts, they can be found roasted in their shells and sold as snacks. For cooking, purchase raw peanuts which are shelled but still retain their skins.

Rosemary
The needle-like leaves of this herb have a fragrant woodsy aroma. Rosemary pairs well with poultry and meat, especially if they are roasted. It is available fresh or dried. Fresh rosemary can keep for up to 10 days wrapped in a damp paper towel and stored in the refrigerator.

Star Anise
This star-shaped spice comes from the fruit of the star anise tree that is native to southwest China. It has a liquorice-like flavour that goes well with poultry and meat. Star anise is often used in Chinese braised dishes. It is also featured in many spice blends used in South East Asian cooking.

Tamarind Paste
This sticky and fibrous dark brown paste comes from the pod-like tamarind fruit, also known as *asam*. It is most commonly sold in blocks but can also be found in jars. Tamarind paste is used as a souring agent in many Asian cuisines.

Thyme
Thyme is a small-leafed and woody-stemmed herb used in many cuisines as it complements a variety of meats, poultry and vegetables. It has a pungent woodsy flavour that is slightly sweet. When whole sprigs of thyme are used in cooking, they should be removed before serving because of their tough stems.

Water Chestnut
The water chestnut is the fleshy root stem of an aquatic plant. When it is peeled and exposed to air, its white flesh will discolour quickly. Soak cut pieces in cold water to prevent discolouration. Being sweet and crisp, water chestnuts can be eaten raw but are often added to cooked dishes for texture.

Wood Ear Fungus
Also known as black fungus or tree ear fungus, this is an edible fungus that ranges in colour from dark brown to black. It is often sold dried and has to be soaked in water to rehydrate before using. It is mostly flavourless and is used to add a crunchy texture to dishes it is used in.

Weights and Measures

Quantities for this book are given in Metric and American (spoon and cup) measures. Standard spoon and cup measurements used are: 1 teaspoon = 5 ml, 1 tablespoon = 15 ml, 1 cup = 250 ml. All measures are level unless otherwise stated.

LIQUID AND VOLUME MEASURES

Metric	Imperial	American
5 ml	1/6 fl oz	1 teaspoon
10 ml	1/3 fl oz	1 dessertspoon
15 ml	1/2 fl oz	1 tablespoon
60 ml	2 fl oz	1/4 cup (4 tablespoons)
85 ml	2 1/2 fl oz	1/3 cup
90 ml	3 fl oz	3/8 cup (6 tablespoons)
125 ml	4 fl oz	1/2 cup
180 ml	6 fl oz	3/4 cup
250 ml	8 fl oz	1 cup
300 ml	10 fl oz (1/2 pint)	1 1/4 cups
375 ml	12 fl oz	1 1/2 cups
435 ml	14 fl oz	1 3/4 cups
500 ml	16 fl oz	2 cups
625 ml	20 fl oz (1 pint)	2 1/2 cups
750 ml	24 fl oz (1 1/5 pints)	3 cups
1 litre	32 fl oz (1 3/5 pints)	4 cups
1.25 litres	40 fl oz (2 pints)	5 cups
1.5 litres	48 fl oz (2 2/5 pints)	6 cups
2.5 litres	80 fl oz (4 pints)	10 cups

DRY MEASURES

Metric	Imperial
30 grams	1 ounce
45 grams	1 1/2 ounces
55 grams	2 ounces
70 grams	2 1/2 ounces
85 grams	3 ounces
100 grams	3 1/2 ounces
110 grams	4 ounces
125 grams	4 1/2 ounces
140 grams	5 ounces
280 grams	10 ounces
450 grams	16 ounces (1 pound)
500 grams	1 pound, 1 1/2 ounces
700 grams	1 1/2 pounds
800 grams	1 3/4 pounds
1 kilogram	2 pounds, 3 ounces
1.5 kilograms	3 pounds, 4 1/2 ounces
2 kilograms	4 pounds, 6 ounces

OVEN TEMPERATURE

	°C	°F	Gas Regulo
Very slow	120	250	1
Slow	150	300	2
Moderately slow	160	325	3
Moderate	180	350	4
Moderately hot	190/200	370/400	5/6
Hot	210/220	410/440	6/7
Very hot	230	450	8
Super hot	250/290	475/550	9/10

LENGTH

Metric	Imperial
0.5 cm	1/4 inch
1 cm	1/2 inch
1.5 cm	3/4 inch
2.5 cm	1 inch